In the War

Food and Rations

Peter Hicks

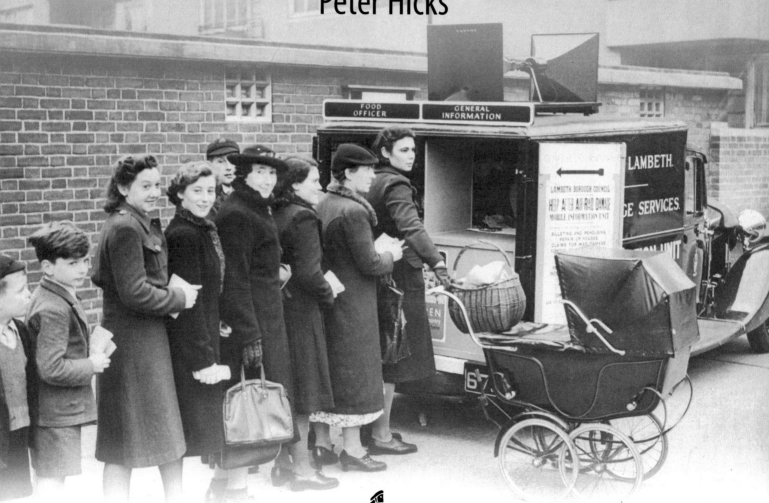

D0452889

First published in 2008 by Wayland

Copyright © Wayland 2008

This paperback edition published in 2010 by Wayland

Wayland
338 Euston Road
London NW1 3BH

Wayland Australia
Level 17/207 Kent Street
Sydney, NSW 2000

Editor: Camilla Lloyd
Designer: Phipps Design
Picture researcher: Shelley Noronha

Acknowledgments:
All Inside Stories from 'Interview with the author' with the exception of p.15 from *How We Lived Then* by Norman Longmate (Hutchinson, 1971) p.474; p.19 from *How We Lived Then* by N. Longmate p.385, p.20 from *How We Lived Then* by N. Longmate p.282, p.25 from *How We Lived Then* by N. Longmate p.301.

Picture Acknowledgments: The author and publisher would like to thank the following for their pictures to be reproduced in this publication: Cover photographs: Wayland Picture Library (both); © Bettman/Corbis: 1, 8, © Hulton-Deutsch Collection/Corbis: 22, 23, 24, 27, 29; Imperial War Museum: 28; Heritage Images/Topfoto: 11, 14; Topfoto: 5, 15, 16, 17, 18, 25, 26; Peter Hicks: 4, 10, 12 (all); Wayland Picture Library: 6, 7, 9, 13, 19, 20, 21.

British Library Cataloguing in Publication Data:
Hicks, Peter, 1952-
    Food and rations. - (In the war)
    1. Rationing - Great Britain - History - 20th century -
    Juvenile literature 2. World War, 1939-1945 - Food supply -
    Juvenile literature 3. World War, 1939-1945 - Social aspects -
    Great Britain - Juvenile literature
    I. Title
    941'.084

ISBN: 978 0 7502 6160 9

Printed in China

Wayland is a division of Hachette Children's Books, an Hachette UK company
www.hachette.co.uk

Contents

Stand firm and united

At 11.15, on the morning of Sunday 3rd September, 1939, the British Prime, Minister Neville Chamberlain, announced to the nation that Britain was 'at war with Germany'. Two days earlier, the German army had invaded Poland, in Eastern Europe. Britain had promised to protect Poland's freedom so Neville Chamberlain had no choice but to declare war.

Germany's invasion of Poland was the spark that led to war, but relations between the two countries had not been good for some time. Germany had been expanding her borders since 1935 taking over more and more land. When her planes and tanks swept into Poland, Britain, and Britain's main ally, France, believed Germany had gone too far.

This poster shows that Britain would need to rely on home-grown food and not imports from abroad.

USE SPADES NOT SHIPS

GROW YOUR OWN FOOD
AND SUPPLY YOUR OWN COOKHOUSE

Think about
How might you have felt that Sunday knowing that some of your family would be called up to fight in the war?

INSIDE STORY:

'For the sake of all that we ourselves hold dear...I now call my people at home and my people across the seas... to stand firm and united in the time of trial.'

Broadcast of King George VI to the nation, 3rd September, 1939.

The fact that Britain was an island made people feel more secure. The English Channel, the 21 mile stretch of water between Britain and Europe, had kept invaders out in the past. However, being an island was both a strength and a weakness because Britain imported 60% of her food from abroad. Germany would take advantage of this weakness as she had done in World War I (1914-18), and send submarines (U-Boats) to sink as many ships as possible. A German U-Boat **blockade** could starve Britain into surrender. Britain would have to produce as much food at home as possible. For Britain to win the war, ships coming in would have to carry war essentials like **ammunition**, guns, tanks and aircraft parts. There would be little room for food.

For safety, ships had to cross the Atlantic in groups, or convoys, protected by British warships like this one.

That's yer lot!

The government knew that Britain's success in the war depended on its ability to feed the **civilian** population. The workforce kept the wheels of industry turning, producing the guns, ships and ammunition for the war. On the 8 January 1940, food rationing was introduced. Rationing meant that each person in Britain was only allowed a fixed amount of certain foods. Food was precious and had to last. Also rationing was fair as everybody was guaranteed a certain amount.

Hungry evacuees from the East End of London enjoy a 3d (1p) meal.

INSIDE STORY:

'My favourite before the war had been banana sandwiches. Well, bananas just disappeared, along with most imported fruits like oranges. So my Mum boiled up some turnips, mashed them and put some banana essence drops in. They weren't too bad.'

Everyone was given a ration book, which you took with you when you went shopping. Each week was numbered and when you bought your rations for that week, the shopkeeper marked your book. Throughout 1940, essential foods were gradually added to the rationed list. You can see in the panel (right), what the weekly ration was by 1942.

The remarkable thing about rationing was that with it the government had introduced a more **balanced diet** to the nation. There were proteins, fats, vitamins and minerals, which were all necessary for a strong workforce and healthy children.

This was the basic weekly ration, with the important ration book.

Weekly food rations (end 1942)

- 113g (4 oz) bacon or ham
- 1s 2d (6p) meat
- 57g (2 oz) butter
- 113g (4 oz) cheese
- 113g (4 oz) margarine
- 113g (4 oz) cooking fat
- 226g (8 oz) sugar
- 57g (2 oz) tea
- 1lb of jam or marmalade every two months

For milk and eggs the amount varied with supply:

- 2½ pints of milk per week and a tin of dried skimmed milk every month
- 1 egg per week and one tin of dried egg every month
- 340g (12 oz) sweets per month

Think about

With your parent's or carer's permission, cut 113g (4 oz) of cheese. Can you make it last a week?

The queues are awfully long!

For a single person, the weekly ration was difficult to live on. Families who had up to four or five ration books could put together their food and make it go further. Many foods were not rationed, but shoppers found these foods could be hard to find. Fish was the most sought after food and fish shop queues were very long! The Ministry of Food, the government department that organized rationing, tried to get shoppers to try new foods. However, most people did not like the idea of whale meat!

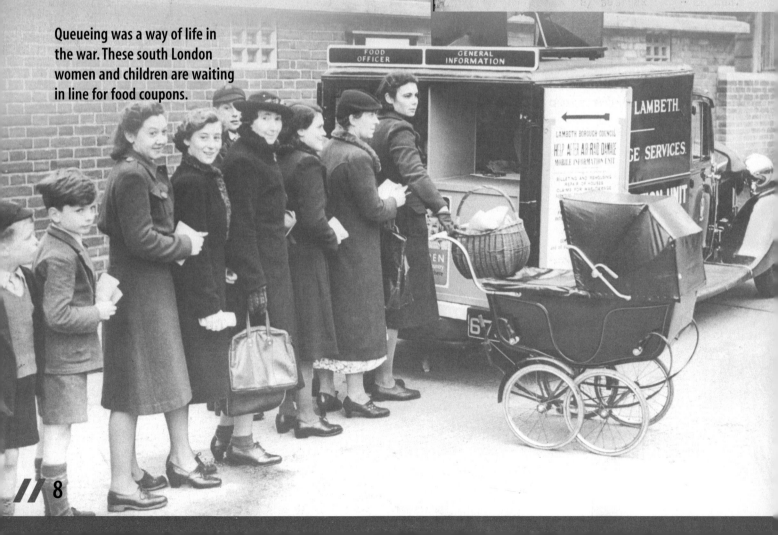

Queueing was a way of life in the war. These south London women and children are waiting in line for food coupons.

Offal – the intestines and internal organs of animals – became very popular but were also hard to find. People experimented with liver, kidney, heart, tongue, pigs' trotters, brains, tripe (intestines) and sheep heads! Sausages were not rationed but many people were suspicious of their contents and found much of the 'meat' was actually bread.

A popular change to rationing came in December 1941, when the Ministry of Food announced the 'points rationing scheme'. Everyone with a ration book was given 16 points (later 20) every month to use at any shop that had the food they wanted. The advantage of this system was that food started appearing in the shops that had not been around for a long time. Spam (spiced ham) in tins was a great hit.

The government encouraged people to eat out once a month. Most popular were the 'British Restaurants' where people could buy a simple dinner – meat, two vegetables, a pudding, bread, butter and tea or coffee for a reasonable 11d (4½p)!

This greengrocer was so fed up about being asked for bananas that he put up this famous sign!

Think about

Why do you think sausages contained so much bread during the war?

Dig for Victory!

On the 4th October 1939, the Ministry of Agriculture began a campaign that became one of the great success stories of the war. The minister, Sir Reginald Smith, pointed out that half a million **allotments** would provide potatoes and vegetables for one and a half million people for eight months. 'So, let's get going. Let "Dig for Victory" be the motto of everyone.'

INSIDE STORY:

'Our next door neighbour was a really good gardener and he had a lovely allotment – he used to spend hours on it. He was very generous. We would always find a pile of vegetables outside our back door.'

It was agriculture and farming that kept the nation fed during the war with increased mechanization, chemical fertilizers, more ploughed land and the work of the **Women's Land Army**. However, the 'Dig for Victory!' campaign was also very important. Huge amounts of food were produced by people of all ages and everyone felt like they were contributing to the war effort.

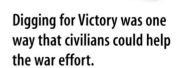

DIG FOR VICTORY

Digging for Victory was one way that civilians could help the war effort.

London had some very unusual allotments, for example the moat of the Tower of London and the royal parks all became allotments. They appeared in recreation grounds, rubbish tips and even bombsites. Most schools set up an allotment and children were keen to join in, especially if it meant missing lessons! Even people without gardens grew tomatoes in window boxes and ornamental tubs.

Where did people learn the skills to grow food? Local gardening societies spread the word and the Ministry of Agriculture provided free leaflets, 'How to Dig' and 'How to Crop'. Millions listened to a weekly radio programme with Mr. Middleton who shared his gardening knowledge.

As well as vegetables, some people reared animals, such as pigs and fed them on kitchen waste. In fact, 'pig clubs' were very popular and a five shilling investment could lead to people getting a good amount of meat when the pig was killed.

Potato and carrot peelings were collected to fatten up the pigs!

Think about
Why do you think many people kept chickens in their back gardens?

SAVE KITCHEN WASTE TO FEED THE PIGS!

THANKS

KEEP IT DRY, FREE FROM GLASS, METAL, BONES, PAPER ETC.

KITCHEN WASTE

IT ALSO FEEDS POULTRY ... *Your Council will collect*

Printed for H.M. Stationery Office by Wm. Brown & Co. Ltd. London, E.C.3 51-2333

S.P. 52.

Have you tried dried eggs yet?

Many ships bringing supplies from the USA were sunk by German U-Boats during 1941-43, so rations could not increase. The Ministry of Food ran a successful campaign to make the ordinary food in the shops interesting and healthy. Housewives were told that vegetables, which were not rationed filled you up and were very good for you.

The colourful characters 'Potato Pete' and 'Dr. Carrot' were created and were seen all over newspapers, magazines and billboards. 'Potato Pete', a cuddly, humorous character announced he was 'low in fat and full of energy.' 'Dr. Carrot' was the 'children's best friend.' His life-giving properties were carried in his bag marked Vit.A (Vitamin A – which improves your eyesight and was supposed to help you to see in a **blackout**!).

See what a lot of nice new friends I've made already

Produced and issued by The Ministry of

DOCTOR CARROT the Children's best friend

VIT-A

TURN OVER A NEW LEAF
Eat Vegetables daily to enjoy good health

Colourful posters encouraged people to cook with a whole range of vegetables.

Think about
Can you find out what Woolton pie was?

The man behind the campaign was the Minister of Food, Lord Woolton. He knew how to use the **media**. There were 'Food Fact' adverts, recipes in magazines and 'Food Flashes' in between films at the cinema. The 'Kitchen Front' radio programme at 8.15 every morning was popular. Useful food facts were given out, often by two **music hall** stars of the day, Gert and Daisy. When told how good milk was for her, especially her teeth, Daisy joked about her false teeth 'You don't say! I'd better put me teeth in a glass of milk tonight!'

When tins of dried egg came from America in 1942, many people thought they tasted rubbery. A suspicious public had to be won over. Adverts saying 'Have YOU tried DRIED EGGS yet?' were published and when recipes for 'Dried Egg and Potato Fritters' appeared in the magazine *Good Housekeeping* it announced that the 'Ministry of Food has approved this article'.

The food campaign during the war educated people about the importance of vitamins.

INSIDE STORY:

'During high summer when all the fruits were ripening, the government gave out a bonus of an extra pound of sugar to help with jam-making. That was very welcome.'

Got any gum, chum?

For children, sweet rationing during the war was very annoying! At first they were allowed 227g (8 oz), then 454g (16 oz), but later the allowance dropped to 340g (12 oz) a month. Four weeks was a very long time to make your chocolate or boiled sweets last.

Most children agreed that the taste of chocolate during the war was less smooth and much more powdery. Also, because milk was in short supply a lot more chocolate produced was plain chocolate rather than milk chocolate and this was not to everybody's taste. Cool ice cream, which was nice on a hot summer's day, also disappeared for the duration of the war.

There were ways to add to the supply of sweets. You could ask people who didn't eat sweets for their ration points. Or Mums could save up some sugar, milk and butter and make home-made fudge. After 1942, if you had US soldiers **billeted** near your house then you were lucky! They were generous with their 'candy': Hershey bars and chewing gum. When children saw the US soldiers, they would call out 'Got any gum, chum?' It became a catch phrase!

This slogan was so famous that it was the inspiration for a successful pop song.

Think about
Which sweets would you miss the most?

INSIDE STORY:

'I lived in Ipswich and was invited to a dance at a nearby American airbase. It was wonderful! During the intervals we had fresh coffee, American-style doughnuts and a huge dish of ice cream. Best of all were the fresh oranges. I took mine home!'

Christmas was a difficult time for children who had to accept that their presents would not be very special. Letters to Santa Claus had the words 'any little thing you can spare.' Turkeys were not available, but families near the countryside could sometimes get hold of a chicken. The Ministry of Food helped with Christmas recipes: 'Wartime Christmas Pudding, made with grated carrots'! One boy sadly remembered receiving a tie and a coat hanger during one particularly hard Christmas.

American soldiers put on a Christmas party for 200 children. Father Christmas arrived by tank!

Don't you know there's a war on?

Of course, it was not only food that was in short supply. All of British industry was geared towards the war effort. As the government said: 'Munitions must come first... This means a sacrifice of comforts...' The shortage of these comforts made life very difficult. For example, crockery was rationed and only three shapes of cup were allowed. Knife and fork production was cut by 75% and teaspoons vanished. Saucepans were rare and many people had to manage with just one.

Furniture was a problem, as timber was in short supply and no longer imported. There were only 22 furniture items that were allowed to be made. People who had been bombed-out or were newly married were given 30 units of 'Utility' furniture – a table was six units and a double bed, five. Utility furniture was 'cheap and cheerful' but it was still remarkably popular.

Although the sign says 'no cigarettes' this shopkeeper obviously keeps some under the counter for his regular customers.

INSIDE STORY:

'You would be walking down the street and you'd see a queue. You had no idea what it was for but you quickly took your place. You'd then ask someone what they were buying. It was bound to be useful. We all did it!'

Men who shaved struggled. Razor blades were so rare that blunted blades had to be used for months. Even soap, the most basic comfort was rationed – 85g (3 oz) of bathroom soap a month – and had to be used sparingly!

Smokers and drinkers had a frustrating war. Cigarettes and alcohol were not rationed but supplies often ran out. A desperate smoker running into a **tobacconist** often saw the assistant wearing a sign 'Sorry, no cigarettes' round his or her neck! Beer was sometimes available but people complained of its weakness.

All available coal and gas were diverted to the war effort and heating and hot water suffered. Posters asked people to save coal to help build **Destroyers**. Signs in hotel bathrooms read: '…You are asked NOT to exceed 5 inches of water in this bathroom…'

Dramatic posters made people who wasted fuel feel guilty and unpatriotic.

Think about
Which shortage would you find the most annoying?

Defeat the Squander Bug and Save!

Life was tough with rationing and the shortages, but many people were reasonably well-off. Most people worked longer hours and wages increased. The government was worried that if people wasted money on non-essentials, the war effort would suffer.

In 1943, a campaign was introduced designed to shame people against wasting money. A character called the 'Squander Bug' was seen in newspapers and magazines. He was a hairy, evil-looking insect and he wanted everyone to waste money. 'Spend it here the prices are fantastic!' he would whisper. The message was clear that if you didn't save money you were helping Germany.

The government organized a savings campaign and encouraged people to 'Hit back with National Savings!' National Savings Certificates were very attractive. Priced at 15 shillings (75p), if you kept them for 10 years they would be worth 20 shillings and 6d (£1.2½p).

The 'Squander Bug' was covered in Nazi Germany's swastika signs so everyone knew he was on the enemy's side.

Think about

Even though times were tough during the war, why did so many people save?

Savings Groups sprung up, which made it easier to save. Running a group was a good way to help with the war effort and they appealed to mothers with babies. Nearly every school had a group and across the country there were 80,000 in many factories, offices and shops.

Various 'campaign weeks' raised money for the armed forces. Children found these weeks exciting because they could meet war heroes or see shot-down German planes displayed. Overall the campaigns raised a massive £2,777 million for the war effort!

INSIDE STORY:

'In our London office after an air-raid we all put in a penny and guessed the time of the next one. If someone guessed correctly, they won the kitty. If we were all wrong the money went to the Spitfire fund.'

Can you see from the posters which weapons this school in Kent were saving up for?

Saucepans into Spitfires

'The Minister of Aircraft Production is asking the women of Great Britain for everything made of aluminium, everything they can possibly give to be made into aeroplanes – Spitfires, Hurricanes, Blenheims and Wellingtons.' This announcement by Lady Reading, the head of the Women's Voluntary Services (WVS) on 19th July 1940, began the most famous **salvage** campaign of the war. Everybody was encouraged to collect scrap metal, especially aluminium that would be melted down and used for **armaments**.

INSIDE STORY:

'*When the collector came to the door I gave him my Mum's best saucepans and lids, our bath tub made of zinc and my Dad's shovel. My Mum "did her nut" and I was quickly sent to the depot to try to find them.*'

This mountain of aluminium saucepans were melted down to be made into aircraft frames.

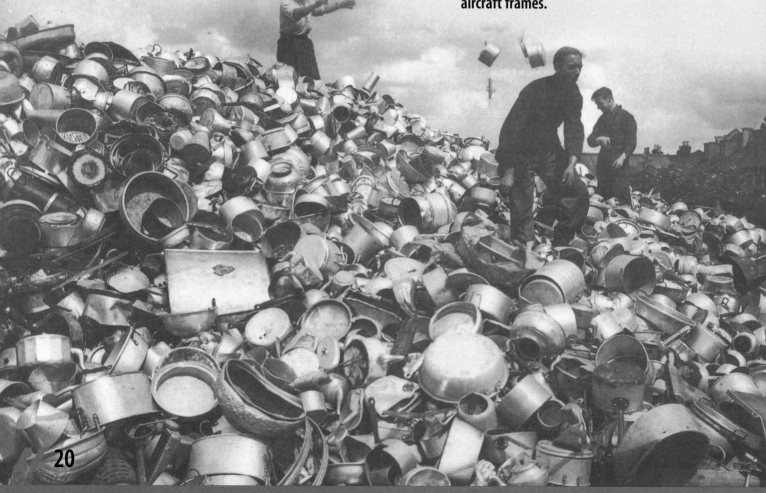

Children were keen to help and they searched for spare pots and pans that could be turned into fighter planes. Amazingly, in the two months of the campaign, 1,000 tons of metal was collected.

Between June 1940 and June 1941 Britain stood alone against Germany and salvage became even more important. Everyone recycled for survival. Households, encouraged by the Ministry of Supplies, had bins for pigswill (waste food), paper, tins, glass jars and bottles. Enthusiastic children or members of the WVS collected this regularly.

Everything from old rubber tyres to milk bottle tops were collected and recycled. 'Enough aluminium to build 50 Lancaster bombers is lost each year through aluminium milk bottle caps being thrown away' claimed a Ministry poster. An amazing 50 million unwanted books were pulped and by 1943, half of the paper used in Britain was home-produced.

Once again people had to be reminded that food was Britain's greatest resource.

The Ministry of Works was in charge of scrap metal and they were collecting 110,000 tons a week in 1943! Most of this came from the removal of railings that surrounded parks, squares and gardens up and down the country.

Think about
Why do you think metal in particular was needed for the war effort?

Make Do and Mend

On 1st June 1941, the government made an announcement that shocked millions of Britons. Clothes were to be rationed! Even the Prime Minister, Winston Churchill did not agree, but the measure was still introduced.

Why was it done? The civilian clothing industry was seen as a waste of resources. The workers could be doing much more worthwhile jobs for the war effort; raw materials could be saved for more important things; and if cotton was not imported the space saved in ships could be used for munitions.

The government brought in 'Utility Clothing'. This new style contained restricted amounts of material and very little trimmings. Skirts tended to be shorter – a way of saving cloth. In the first year, everyone had 66 coupons for clothes, but by the second year this was 60 coupons and had to last 15 months. By 1945, it had dropped to 41. Some people liked the 'Utility' look but others thought it drab and dreary.

The government would rather you did not spend your money on new clothes; so 'Mrs. Sew and Sew' was introduced whose motto was 'Make Do and Mend'. The message was that

These old stockings were used to keep airmen warm and bandages clean.

Think about
Why do you think Utility skirts had so few pleats?

if your clothes were old or torn don't buy new clothes, but mend the old ones. The WVS set up the useful Children's Clothing Exchange Centres where mothers could exchange clothes for larger or smaller sizes.

The Board of Trade tried to encourage children to 'do their bit' and published two helpful posters; 'Useful jobs that girls can do to help win the war' and 'Simple jobs boys can do themselves and so help win the war.' The slogan was:'Mend and restore, and you can lend more'.

INSIDE STORY:

'I remember, when I came home on leave I wanted to buy some trousers with turn-ups, which was the fashion. Utility trousers didn't allow turn-ups (they wasted material) so I bought longer trousers and got my wife to sew in the turn-ups!'

Make Do and Mend. These boys were being taught how to darn socks.

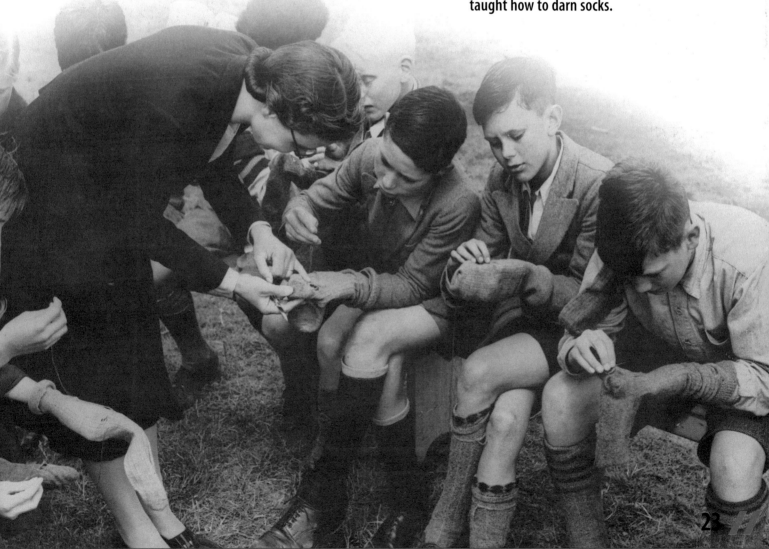

our journey really necessary?

During the 1930s and 1940s, only a small percentage of the population owned a car so the majority relied on public transport. The war put the transport system under great pressure, especially the railways. Many train services were taken over by the military so for civilians travelling by train was often uncomfortable and sometimes dangerous.

A railway post told passengers as they entered the station: 'Food, shells and fuel must come first.' The overstretched railways carried out amazing things. It helped to **evacuate** millions of children during 1939-40. Later, when the army was sent to North Africa, 1,100 trains took them to the ports on the south coast to sail there. During 1941-42, 1,700 goods trains shifted 75,000 tons of London's bomb-damaged rubble to Norfolk and Suffolk to build runways for the **Bomber Command**.

A clever way of getting servicemen home on leave was by sharing lifts in cars.

Think about
Why do you think civilian trains were so slow during the war?

Normal civilian travellers were often forgotten. In 1940, station names were even removed because of an invasion scare and many travellers got lost! Trains and stations were bombed or machine-gunned and altogether, 900 people were killed on the railways during the war.

Petrol rationing began on 22nd September 1939. The amount received depended on the size of the car and the basic rate varied between 4 to 10 gallons a month. This represented roughly 120 miles of driving. Petrol used for domestic consumption was called **pool** costing 1s 6d a gallon (7½p). In 1942, the basic rate had to be stopped (because of the petrol shortage) and as a result there were far less cars on the road. Coupons were issued for essential travel, but if you were caught driving without a proper purpose you could be imprisoned.

This poster was on display in every railway station booking office.

INSIDE STORY:

'*Overcrowding was a problem. I remember travelling home for Christmas and the train stopped at Coventry where hundreds of munition workers piled on. There were wooden tables between the seats so some of them just picked them up and threw them out of the window to make room to stand!*'

It fell off the back of a lorry

Although people accepted rationing, some were prepared to pay extra for items that they couldn't get. Obtaining a rationed item illegally was called 'buying on the black market.' Having put up with shortages for so long, people were often tempted to buy things they really wanted. The black market was small scale but there were organized gangs of criminals who tried to make money by selling illegal goods.

Where did the black market goods come from? They were stolen. Criminals would target a warehouse containing clothes or petrol coupons. They might break in on a Friday and put a new lock on the door, so it wouldn't be noticed until Monday. By that time, the goods were in London and being sold illegally.

'Bootleggers' or 'spivs' sold a whole range of illegal goods on the Black Market.

DON'T BE A BOOTLEGGER

Are You a Wartime Chiseler? The Boys at the Front Aren't!

By ROLLIN KIRBY

Famous American cartoonist, who offers here the eighth in his series of cartoons for LOOK

The "Black Market" is open for business, and unhappy days are here again.

Once more the bootlegger, that malodorous spawn of Prohibition, is on the prowl. Liquor, once the Golconda into which the criminal world dug so deeply, has been replaced by gasoline, tire, coffee and food coupons.

The average good citizen gladly accepts the restrictions set up by the Government to keep our troops properly fed, equipped and trans...ported. But not everyone is a good citizen. The rats are active again.

This whole bootlegging process is a cor...rupting one—for the buyer as well as the seller is guilty of sabotaging the war effort.

So far, bootlegging has not reached the hijacking-murder stage. But it will if the law does not control it with a heavy...

It was easy for rationed goods to be stolen from the London docks because they were such busy places that the thieves went unnoticed. A lorry might drive in to pick up 100 sides of pork. The driver might know the **tally-man**, give him the 'wink', and 110 sides of pork would be put in the lorry. On his way to the meat market the driver might drop the extra 10 off to black market sellers. If anyone asked where it came from, the reply was, 'It fell off the back of a lorry.'

The railways suffered from theft as well. In 1941, the four main railway companies lost £1 million worth of goods (£15 million in today's money). The worst robbery during the war was at Romford in Essex, when £500,000 worth of clothing coupons were stolen. These were quickly sold on the black market.

Cosmetics were very difficult to find during the war. Some people made fake perfume and make-up and sold them in shops.

Think about
What would you be most tempted to buy on the black market during the war?

A long, hard road

The war against Germany ended in May 1945 and the war against Japan in August. Victory celebrations sprang up all over the country but things did not get better immediately. Britain had become **bankrupt** as a result of nearly 6 years of **total war**. The new Prime Minister, Clement Atlee, admitted the country was in serious financial trouble. As a result, food imports would have to be cut. Goods would have to be exported to make money for Britain, so there would be even less to buy in the shops. All this came as a huge shock to the population who, as we have seen, had made huge sacrifices during the war.

By 1946, because of a terrible world food shortage, the government continued rationing. Butter, margarine and cooking fat were cut to 198g (7 oz) a week and bread was rationed. In 1947, the meat ration was cut to 1 shilling's worth (5p) and government posters warned 'Export or Die' and 'Work or Want.' The tinned meat ration was cut to 2d (1p) a week, although the sweet ration went up to 142 g (5 oz).

mother don't forget baby's COD LIVER OIL AND ORANGE JUICE

School dinners, brought in during the war, as well as cheap milk, orange juice, cod liver oil, vitamins and extra eggs made children healthier and stronger.

Think about
Why do you think people were so disappointed that rationing carried on after the war?

A 'Victory in Europe' (VE-Day) party in South London, May 1945. The tables were 'V'-shaped!

Despite all this hardship, the nation's health actually improved during the 1940s. Rationing brought a balanced diet for everyone and made children stronger and healthier. The proof was in the infant mortality rate (the death rate of children up to the age of five). In 1938, it was 56 per 1,000 births. By 1946, it had dropped to 45.

It had been a long, hard road but things eventually improved and all rationing ended in July 1954. The sweet ration ended on 5th February 1953!

INSIDE STORY:

'I had been in London on VE Day [Victory in Europe Day] attending a concert at the Royal Albert Hall with friends. The streets were full of people walking in all directions. When we went back to Brighton by train there were bonfires burning at towns and villages all along the track, glowing in the dark. It was wonderful.'

Timeline

- **3 September 1939** — Germany invades Poland and WWII starts.

- **22 September 1939** — Petrol is rationed.

- **8 January 1940** — Butter, sugar, bacon and ham rationing begins.

- **11 March 1940** — Meat rationing begins.

- **19 July 1940** — Scrap metal collections begin.

- **3 December 1940** — Lord Woolton (Food Minister) announces an increase in sugar and tea rations for Christmas.

- **2 June 1941** — Clothes rationing begins.

- **4 July 1941** — Coal is rationed.

- **15 December 1941** — The government aims to quadruple the amount of scrap metal collected.

- **2 February 1941** — Rosehip syrup goes on sale. Over two million children receive free cod liver oil.

- **25 October 1942** — Sugar on the top of cakes is forbidden.

- **8 May 1945** — Victory in Europe Day.

- **15 March 1949** — Clothes rationing ends.

- **3 May 1950** — Petrol rationing ends.

- **3 July 1954** — Food rationing ends.

Glossary

Air-raid When enemy aircraft dropped bombs on towns and cities.

Allotments Plots of land where you could grow fruit and vegetables.

Ammunition or munitions A supply of bullets, shells, bombs and grenades for the armed forces.

Armaments Weapons of war, such as guns and tanks.

Balanced diet Diet with the right amount of carbohydrates, protein, fat, minerals and fibre.

Bankrupt When a country or person runs out of money.

Billeted When evacuees or soldiers are lodged in private houses.

Blackout When lights were put out to protect people and buildings from attack.

Blockade Stopping the entry of important goods into a country.

Bomber Command The section of the British Royal Air Force containing all the heavy bomber aircraft.

Civil Service The government departments that run the country.

Civilian Someone who is not in the armed forces.

Destroyers Light, fast warships that protect other ships from enemy attack.

Evacuate To move away from an area that might be dangerous.

Media Newspapers and broadcasting that gives information to the population.

Music hall A place of entertainment with dancers, singers and comedians.

Pool A blend of petrol that replaced other types and was for civilian use.

Salvage The saving and re-use of waste paper or scrap metal.

Tally-man A person who counts the number of goods entering and leaving a port.

Tobacconist A person who sells cigarettes, tobacco, pipes and matches.

Total War War in which everyone is involved.

Women's Land Army Organization of women who worked on farms because there was a shortage of farm workers.

Further information

Books to read

In the War: School Life by Peter Hicks (Wayland, 2008)

In the War: The Blitz by Simon Adams (Wayland, 2008)

In the War: Evacuation by Simon Adams (Wayland, 2008)

Britain at War : Rationing by Martin Parsons (Wayland, 1999)

William at War by Richmal Crompton (Macmillan Children's Books, 1995)

Websites

http://www.bbc.co.uk/history/worldwars/wwtwo BBC history site on WWII.

http://www.bbc.co.uk/dna/h2g2/A533918 Detailed site on rationing.

Index

Numbers in **bold** refer to pictures and captions.